I0456489

PAIGE WILLIAMS

THE DISCIPLES MANUAL

ACCORDING TO THE GOSPELS
MATTHEW & LUKE

The Disciples Manual: According to the gospels Matthew & Luke

Paige Michael Williams

Copyright © 2024

All rights reserved. This book is protected by the copyright laws of the United States of America. This book may not be copied or reprinted for commercial gain or profit. The use of short quotations or occasional page copying for personal or group study is permitted and encouraged. Permission will be granted upon request.

All definitions courtesy of ©Cambridge University Press & Assessment 2024 https://dictionary.cambridge.org/us/

Published by Seraph Creative in 2024

United States / United Kingdom / South Africa / Australia

www.seraphcreative.org

All rights reserved. No part of this book, artwork included, may be used or reproduced in any matter without the written permission of the publisher.

ISBN 978-1-958997-81-9

CONTENTS

DISCIPLES MANUAL

It was an early morning in October and I was shut away in prayer and meditation on the Lord. My eyes were closed as I was thinking of the Lord, and then I saw a vision. In this vision, the Lord Jesus was walking and His back was to me, and my first reaction was to try and see His Face, but at first, I could not. Then the vision faded, and a few moments later another vision appeared, and again Jesus was walking with His back facing me, but this time I saw a hand that reached out to Him and touched His left shoulder, and He turned and I saw His Face! There was such a humility, yet sincerity in His eyes that pierced through my soul. There was meekness in His expression but it was coupled with such resolution and fire. Yet with a willingness to listen and hear what I had to say. His Face exuded endless passionate love for us that I cannot describe. Then as quickly as it appeared, the vision faded and He was gone.

There was a wealth of revelation being downloaded into my spirit man as these visions took place. You see, Jesus Himself is a revelation, His very presence and existence exudes revelation. But we need the Spirit of wisdom and understanding (Isaiah 11:2) to illuminate the mysteries of Christ that are revealed in His appearances. To put it plainly this was a revelation of the heart of Jesus in this season that we are in, yet this has always been His heart since He walked the earth over two thousand years ago. Through these visions, I was able to see part of what the Lord is doing and what He desires us.

Notes

_____

_____

_____

_____

_____

_____

_____

_____

_____

_____

Chapter Glossary

Revelation - the act of making something known that was secret, or a fact that is made known.

Meekness - the quality of being quiet, gentle, and unwilling to argue or express your opinions.

Illuminate - to light something and make it brighter.

Notes

Notes

INTERPRETATION

The first vision reveals that Jesus is moving forward, and if we want to be with Him and see His Face continually, we must follow Him and walk with Him, which is to be a disciple! Jesus is not waiting in this season, this is a season of acceleration. He is moving on as our fearless leader and teacher and we must be wise enough to follow Him. But all those who follow Him must do so willingly, He will not make anyone follow Him. He is meek and lowly in heart, and very humble, so He will not make a big fuss (so to speak) but He is calling all disciples! Jesus tends to call more by what He does than what He says. His actions truly do speak louder than His words, because His words are derived from His heart and intention to do a work. His Word reveals what He already intended in His heart to do. But His word is above His name, so His actions will always be in alignment and under the subjection of His word. They will also magnify and exemplify His Word as true reality, that's why He's called the Living Word.

The second vision was revealing what it would take to be close to Him, touch Him, and see His Face. It is to follow Him, which is the call of the disciples. You will not be able to touch Jesus in a real way without truly following Him, and it is much easier to touch Him when you are close to Him. He is also more willing to give His time to those who have forsaken all to follow and walk with Him. But the greatest reward of following Jesus is to see His face continually and know His heart, to share everlasting intimacy with Him. His face reveals His heart to us without words, His face communicates with us spirit to spirit (deep calling unto deep). We understand Him more in our spirit by beholding His face. You see eternity everlasting is in His face, security and stability are in His face. His eyes speak to us of deep love and passion beyond this world. His very posture captivates you, and makes you want to conform to His Image. His hands are like foundations that hold us together in a world that is falling apart. His feet are inviting, yet firm and established, revealing an endless possibility of hope in following Him. They speak of a journey with Him that is beyond words. Simply put...Follow Him!

Notes

_____

_____

_____

_____

_____

_____

_____

_____

_____

_____

Chapter Glossary

Acceleration - the increase in something's speed, or its ability to go faster.

Subjection - the state of being under the political control of another country or state.

Possibility - a chance that something may happen or be true.

Notes

Notes

THE FOUNDATION

Discipleship is the foundation of all other relationships with The Lord Jesus Christ. Being a disciple means to be a pupil or student of another. To learn from them their way of life and their ways of operation and the heart behind why they do things the way they do them. You must lose interest in yourself and become obsessed with The Lord, our Master and Friend. He must become more important to you than your own life because as a disciple you now live for Him. You have an important calling as a disciple, to love your Master and to be like Him.

In Matthew 4:19 Jesus said unto His disciples, "Follow me; and I will make you fishers of men." The very first command that Jesus gave to his disciples was to follow Him. If we do not follow Him our relationship with Him stops there. Until we get up from where we are presently and follow Him, we will not have true intimacy with The Lord. Nor will we have the fellowship He's designed for us to have with one another. To follow The Lord you are forsaking your life, you are leaving one thing and gaining another. It is an eternal exchange between you and The Lord Jesus.

Notes

_____

_____

_____

_____

_____

_____

_____

_____

_____

_____

Chapter Glossary

Disciple - a person who believes in the ideas of a leader, esp. a religious or political one, and tries to live according to those ideas.

Calling - a strong wish to do a job, usually one that is socially valuable.

Exchange - the act of giving something to someone and them giving you something else.

Notes

Notes

KINGS: THE PURPOSE OF DISCIPLESHIP

What is the primary purpose of discipleship? What is following Jesus leading us into after salvation? The answer is Sonship. But in order to be like the Son of God and walk in the fullness and maturity of Sonship, we must learn our kingship. Kingship brings you into greater intimacy and closeness with Jesus because He is a King. To relate to him in his purpose and destiny that He shared with you, making you a king, just as He is, is to relate to him out of the realm of kingship. We are sitting together with him in Heavenly places. Are we to sit there silent? Absolutely not! We are to have deep fellowship and intimacy with Him from the high places in which we sit, which are our thrones.

When Jesus called his disciples and told them "Follow Me" He was calling them into their kingship. In the beginning, God created man in His image and part of being in the image of God is to be a king. This is what the Blood of Jesus bought back for us. Revelation 1:5-6 says it this way: *"And from **Jesus Christ**, who is the faithful witness, and the first begotten of the dead, and the prince of the kings of the earth. Unto him that loved us, and washed us from our sins in **his own blood**, And hath made us **kings** and priests unto God and his Father; to him be glory and dominion for ever and ever. Amen."*

You see, Jesus' blood paid for and bought your kingship. He purchased your right to rule and reign with Him. This is part of what satan took from Adam, he stole his crown or kingship through deception. Jesus bought it back for us through His death on the cross at Calvary. He died for more than just paying for our sins, He died to make you a king in His Kingdom. Every time a soul is born again of the Spirit of God, the Kingdom of God just expanded. Another throne and another kingdom are added to God's Empire.

Being Jesus' disciple will teach you the ways of The King and His Kingdom. Without true discipleship, you are not operating in the kingdom of God. You may be operating in the church but not in the kingdom. You must understand that the kingdom is the head of the church. The kingdom is eternal; before Jesus ever established the church there was the kingdom. The kingdom birthed the church. The church came out of the kingdom, just as Eve came out of Adam. Adam and Eve were not created in the church but in the kingdom of God, then Jesus came and established the church over two thousand years ago. This is why we are *kings* and *priests,* we're kings in the kingdom and priests in the church. Symbolically, the kingdom (man) is the male and the church (woman), is the female, this is why the church is also called the *bride* of Christ. In the kingdom, we're sons of God and in the church, we're His bride. The kingdom is the government of God, the church is the family of God. So to be a true disciple of Jesus Christ is to be discipled into the kingdom of God and into your kingship. We will never change the world until we walk in our kingship and sonship. That is what Jesus trains disciples to do, change the world! Priests do not change the world, they change the church or the house of God. Kings change the world through divine government, authority and dominion. Ruling their jurisdictions in the stead of God as His appointed kings and authorities in the earth. This is the call of the disciples of Jesus Christ.

Chapter Glossary

Salvation - (a way of) being saved from danger, loss, or harm.

Fellowship - a group of people or an organization with the same purpose.

Eternal - lasting forever or for a very long time.

Notes

Notes

ATTRIBUTES OF DISCIPLES

We will now embark on an in-depth, yet simple study of the attributes of the disciples of Jesus Christ, and we will do this through the scriptures. There are many simple yet profound attributes of the disciples of Jesus Christ revealed throughout the Bible, and we're going to dive into them. My prayer is that you would use them as a measuring tool to gauge the level of your discipleship to the Lord Jesus. That you would be open and honest with yourself in reading them, not only regarding your strengths but also your weaknesses, so that we together can become wholehearted followers and disciples of the Lord Jesus!

"Bind up the testimony, seal the law among

my disciples." (Isaiah 8:16)

Note this is the only scripture in the Old Testament of the Bible that uses the word disciple. Yet this is a powerful and revelatory scripture that with understanding should cause every believer in Christ Jesus to desire to be His disciple. Two major statements are brought to light from this scripture. The first is that the testimony of the Lord is with His disciples and sealed in them. That word testimony speaks of the face-to-face intimate testimonies of the Lord to His disciples, and these are bound (wrapped up) in His disciples. Only the disciples of Jesus Christ can release certain testimonies from the Lord because they are the ones to whom He reveals and seals them. The true disciples of the Lord Jesus receive testimonies from Him, their Teacher, which the ordinary casual believer does not receive. The second statement is a command to seal (close up) the law among his disciples. The law (commandments/government) of God is a revelation of His Ways, so in essence the ways of The Lord are closed up in His disciples. Meaning that the ways of The Lord are alive and a part of their spirit so that they can manifest them. One of the major benefits of being the Lord's disciple is to have His ways (laws) become a part of your innermost being and nature, that's amazing!

Notes

_____

_____

_____

_____

_____

_____

_____

_____

_____

_____

Chapter Glossary

Attributes - a quality or characteristic that someone or something has.

Scripture - the holy writings of a religion.

Commandments - an order, especially one of the Ten Commandments.

Notes

Notes

THE BOOK OF MATTHEW

"*And seeing the multitudes, he went up into a mountain: and when he was set, his disciples came unto him, and he opened his mouth, and taught them, saying...*" (Matthew 5:1-2)

In this scripture we see that Jesus goes up into a mountain, this is symbolic of going higher in the Spirit. And when He was settled, his disciples came unto him. Disciples follow the Lord, they are never far from Him. They actually travel in the Spirit with Him to the heights and depths to which He leads them. Disciples always come to Him, wherever He is and the Lord subsequently begins to teach them from these different realms of the Spirit, and to reveal Kingdom mysteries to them. But there is an amazing revelation hidden in this scripture about the nature of Jesus and the depth of His revelation and teaching. The scripture says that he *opened his mouth* and taught them. So there was also teaching without words. This reveals that a lot of Jesus' teaching didn't come from His mouth or what He was saying, but by His nature and what He was doing. In other words, the character and personality of Jesus taught His disciples just as much as His words. Wow!

"And when he was entered into a ship, his disciples followed him." (Matthew 8:23)

This verse is literally a foundation of the disciple's call. Ships are symbolic of ministries and to enter into the ship with the Lord is to enter into His ministry. The call is never to leave the Master, where He goes, we go. That is the disciples' covenant. It is the vow never to leave the Master and for the Master never to leave us. Now through scripture, we understand that there were times when the Lord went ahead of the disciples and times when he stayed behind. We also will experience short seasons of distance. This is for the sake of growth and maturity in his disciples. To gauge their ability to carry out His commands and what He has taught them up until that point, without feeling His tangible Presence there with them. There will also be stormy seasons on the boat just like the disciples experienced in Matthew 8:24-27, where our faith as disciples will be tested. This is also a part of entering into the ship (ministry) of the Lord Jesus. The best part of being in the Lord's ship is the great seasons of harvest, when we the fishers of men have great success because of following the instructions of the Lord Jesus, just like in *St. Luke 5:4-7* and *St. John 21:6*.

"And his disciples came to him, and awoke him, saying, Lord, save us: we perish. And he saith unto them, Why are ye fearful, O ye of little faith? Then he arose, and rebuked the winds and the sea; and there was a great calm." (Matthew 8:25-26)

We as disciples must be careful and watchful for the deadly enemy of fear in our lives. Even though we dwell close to The Lord we can still live with fear in our hearts. But we have to understand that being with The Lord is safety! Even if He is silent and we cannot see Him or feel Him. He is still with us and is the Master of all things, including our storms.

"And it came to pass, as Jesus sat at meat in the house, behold, many publicans and sinners came and sat down with him and his disciples." (Matthew 9:10)

If we are to mature in Christ, we as disciples must grow and learn with others. We have to learn how to sit at The Lord's table *together*. Whether it be with sinners, new believers, or mature believers, we need to be humble enough to be taught with others, whether they are on "our level" or not. This is a sign of maturity in God.

"And when the Pharisees saw it, they said unto his disciples, Why eateth your Master with publicans and sinners?" (Matthew 9:11)

Disciples must be prepared to defend their Master. We must know Him and His ways well enough to be able to justify Him before the eyes of men beyond reasonable doubt. Even if they don't receive our testimony of Him or our word. The world and unfortunately a great portion of the church will question the ways of Christ, with the intent to belittle or discredit them. But this is where we (His disciples) who know Him, must stand up for Him and justify and sanctify Him before the people.

"Then came to him the disciples of John, saying, Why do we and the Pharisees fast oft, but thy disciples fast not?" (Matthew 9:14)

We as disciples of the Lord Jesus Christ have the privilege and opportunity to walk very closely with Him. To experience an intimacy that many others do not get to experience or receive. In this scripture, the religious leaders of the day were questioning why the disciples didn't fast, as it was customary among the religious leaders and the people of God. Jesus went on to tell them simply, that it was because He was with them! The reason we fast is to become closer to God, but He was with them physically, so in essence they did not need to fast. This is a revelation of the closeness of Jesus to His disciples, that they experience a greater level of intimacy with Him than others do. This is also a revelation of times and seasons for fasting. There are times set by God for us to fast and draw near to Him, then there are times of refreshing and intimacy with The Lord that do not require fasting.

"And Jesus arose, and followed him, and so did his disciples." (Matthew 9:19)

When The Lord is moving so should we. This is a very important part of being a disciple. Which is to be totally open and available to The Lord, to be flexible enough to move when He moves and at His pace. Also to be disciplined enough to stay in place when He is still and dwelling in a certain place. In other words, we must have total and complete trust in His leadership and guidance to be a disciple.

"Then saith he unto his disciples, The harvest truly is plenteous, but the labourers are few; Pray ye therefore the Lord of the harvest, that he will send forth labourers into his harvest." (Matthew 9:37)

This is a great command from The Lord to His disciples. It is a commission to pray for laborers to enter into the harvest that is sent from God. Maybe the reason that there are few true laborers in the harvest is because we have failed to obey this crucial command from The Lord. I strongly believe He was giving us the solution to this problem of only having a few laborers, which is to pray (seek, request, inquire) that God would send forth laborers into His harvest. This is for our own help and benefit. The workload of the Kingdom of Heaven will become much lighter and enjoyable if there is more to labor with us, as opposed to few! This is a need that we His disciples must address through prayer to open up gateways and portals for God to release laborers into the harvest.

"And when he had called unto him his twelve disciples;

he gave them power against unclean spirits, to cast them out, and to heal all manner of sickness and all manner of disease." (Matthew 10:1)

The disciples of the Lord will be given power (authority) by The Lord Jesus to cast out devils and heal all manner of sickness and disease. This is vitally important because with the message of the Kingdom of God should come power (authority) or the demonstration of that Kingdom. Two major ways that it is demonstrated are through the casting out of devils and the healing of the sick. It is a part of the disciple's package to be like their Lord and heal the sick and cast out devils!

"And it came to pass, when Jesus had made an end of commanding his twelve disciples, he departed thence to teach, and to preach in their cities." (Matthew 11:1)

The Lord will often command His disciples to do certain things. This is one of the main foundations of the disciple's call which is to obey their Master, otherwise you are not a disciple at all. This also shows that we must be co-laborers with God. The Lord had commanded the disciples to do their work and he went about to do His work. This is what happens spiritually today. The Lord Jesus will give us a command or instruction to accomplish in the earth and He will go about doing His personal work whether in heaven or in the earth.

"But when the Pharisees saw it, they said unto him, Behold, thy disciples do that which is not lawful to do upon the Sabbath day." (Matthew 12:2)

Disciples will often break down traditions and religion because their pursuit is a living, breathing, person, not just the letter of the law or rules and regulations. They must follow the Lord in spite of what the religious church and denominations have set in place as the way. And as a result of this, they will offend the spiritually dead church, by following the living way!

"And he stretched forth his hand toward his disciples, and said, Behold my mother and my brethren!" (Matthew 12:49)

Disciples will often receive inspiring revelation from the Lord on just who they are to Him. In this passage of scripture, the disciples are called His mother and brethren. We are His mother because we carry Him in us (through His Word or Seed) and as we mature He grows in us. We also carry His Spirit within us and give birth to His fruit, and help in giving birth to other sons of God (which are his brethren). This is also why we are His brethren because like He was, we are born of His Father by The Spirit of God.

"And the disciples came, and said unto him, Why speakest thou unto them in parables?" (Matthew 13:10)

Many times as disciples we will be required to inquire of the ways of The Lord. He will not come out and just say certain things because He wants us to seek Him, and desire to know Him and His ways. But as we seek to know His ways we can rest assured that He will reveal Himself to us, as it is His pleasure to do so.

"And the disciples came, and took the body, and buried it, and went and told Jesus." (Matthew 14:12)

Disciples will have the privilege of performing special tasks for the Lord. This is because the Lord trusts them with the things that are close to Him. This comes from a bond that is built in their relationship with the Lord over time.

"And when it was evening, his disciples came to him, saying, This is a desert place, and the time is now past; send the multitude away, that they may go into the villages, and buy themselves victuals." (Matthew 14:15)

In this passage of scripture, the Lord is about to feed the five thousand by multiplying five loaves of bread and two fishes. Here we see that the disciples of The Lord get a behind-the-scenes view of the Majesty of The Lord in His miraculous works.

"And straightway Jesus constrained his disciples to get into a ship, and to go before him unto the other side of the ship." (Matthew 14:22)

There are times when disciples will be constrained or compelled by The Lord to go and do certain things according to His will, and we must be wise enough to follow His instructions, even without full understanding.

"And when the disciples saw him walking on the sea, they were troubled, saying, It is a spirit; and they cried out for fear." (Matthew 14:26)

As disciples, we will receive new and divine revelations of Jesus that will take us out of our comfort zones. The Lord must shock and awe us in order to stretch and expand our paradigm of who He is and what is available to us through Him, as His disciples.

"Then came his disciples, and said unto him, Knowest thou that the Pharisees were offended, after they heard this saying?" (Matthew 15:12)

Disciples will question the ways of The Lord from time to time. These times are great opportunities for the Lord to teach us His ways and His heart behind His actions. Don't be afraid to ask questions disciples!

"But he answered her not a word. And his disciples came and besought him, saying, Send her away; for she crieth after us." (Matthew 15:23)

Disciples will petition and urge The Lord on certain matters, but in this, we must continue to allow The Lord to lead us and give us understanding.

"Then Jesus called his disciples unto him, and said, I have compassion on the multitude, because they continue with me now three days, and have nothing to eat: and I will not send them away fasting, lest they faint in the way." (Matthew 15:22)

Many times disciples will receive revelation from The Lord of His heart for humanity. When this happens it is also a call to us to sync our hearts with His and take on His passions as our own.

"And when his disciples were come to the other side, they had forgotten to take bread." (Matthew 16:5)

Disciples will sometimes throughout their journey forget the Word of The Lord.

"When Jesus came into the coasts of Caesarea Philippi, he asked his disciples, saying, Whom do men say that I the Son of man am?" (Matthew 16:13)

Disciples will be asked to report matters to the Lord, especially on behalf of others. The Lord will evoke disciples to consider the hearts of the men and women around them and their testimony of Him.

"Then charged he his disciples that they should tell no man that he was Jesus the Christ." (Matthew 16:20)

The disciples of The Lord will be charged by The Lord to keep His secrets. These secrets are revelations of who He is and must be released in the proper time and season. Jesus trusts His disciples with His secrets. This is a great benefit of being a disciple of Jesus Christ.

"From that time forth began Jesus to shew unto his disciples, how that he must go unto Jerusalem, and suffer many things of the elders and chief priests and scribes, and be killed, and be raised again the third day." (Matthew 16:21)

We as His disciples should be receiving the mysteries of the future. If we follow Him closely enough He will release to us the secrets of the future to prepare us, whether they are good or bad.

"Then Jesus said unto his disciples, If any man will come after me, let him deny himself, and take up his cross, and follow me." (Matthew 16:24)

Disciples of The Lord must qualify for this privilege and the qualification is to follow His example. (Which is crucifixion or death to self) If we are not willing to do this, we cannot be His disciples.

"While he yet spake, behold, a bright cloud overshadowed them: and behold a voice out of the cloud, which said, This is my beloved Son, in whom I am well pleased; hear ye him. And when the disciples heard it, they fell on their face, and were sore afraid" (Matthew 17:5-6)

Faithful disciples of Jesus Christ will meet and encounter the Father. The Father of our Lord Jesus Christ is greater than Jesus in rank (St. John 14:28). He is the head of the Godhead and He wants to meet you personally (1 Corinthians 11:3). This is the main purpose of being a disciple of Jesus Christ (The Door) is to be reconciled to The Father (Romans 5:10, 2 Corinthians 5:18-20).

"And his disciples asked him, saying, Why then say the scribes that Elias must first come?" (Matthew 17:10)

Disciples will often ask The Lord for the revelation of the scriptures. This is right and in perfect order seeing that disciples are to learn from their master, who is the Living Word.

"And I brought him to thy disciples, and they could not cure him." (Matthew 17:16)

Disciples will face disappointments and sometimes embarrassment along their journey in following the Lord. But in those times we must draw from the experience and learn what God is trying to teach us.

"At the same time came the disciples unto Jesus, saying, Who is the greatest in the kingdom of heaven?" (Matthew 18:1)

Disciples will have spiritual ambitions and desires from the Lord for their sacrifice in following Him. This is a good thing if we're willing to pay the price for them.

"Then were there brought unto him little children, that he should put his hands on them, and pray: and the disciples rebuked them. (Matthew 19:13)

Many times disciples will get ahead of themselves. Believing that they know more than they really do. But the Lord will correct them in this and teach them balance, humility and patience.

"When his disciples heard it, they were exceedingly amazed, saying, Who then can be saved?" (Matthew 19:25)

The disciples of The Lord will be astonished by His revelatory teaching as they follow Him.

"And Jesus going up to Jerusalem took the twelve disciples apart in the way, and said unto them" (Matthew 20:17)

Jesus will often give personal or private teaching sessions to His disciples. He will invest extra time into them, that he will not invest in the casual believer.

"And when they drew nigh unto Jerusalem, and were come to Bethphage, unto the mount of Olives, then sent Jesus two disciples, Saying unto them, Go into the

village over against you, and straightway ye shall find an ass tied, and a colt with her: loose them , and bring them unto me. And if any man say ought unto you, ye shall say, The Lord hath need of them; and straightway he will send them." (Matthew 21:1-3)

Disciples will play an integral part in fulfilling prophecy. They are the Lord's laborers who lend their efforts to fulfilling God's plan.

"And the disciples went, and did as Jesus commanded them" (Matthew 21:6)

Discipleship requires quick and simple obedience. The submitted heart obeys immediately. It is only the heart that is not fully submitted to the Lord, that wrestles with His Authority.

"And when the disciples saw it, they marvelled, saying, How soon is the fig tree withered away!" (Matthew 21:20)

The Lord's power and authority will cause His disciples to marvel. They will know the secrets of the Lord's hand. Things that many will overlook and pass by not seeing that it was The Lord's doing.

"And Jesus went out, and departed from the temple: and his disciples came to him for to shew him the buildings of the temple." (Matthew 24:1)

Disciples will at times try to impress the Lord with the wrong things. As we continue to walk with Him and know Him better, we learn what really pleases Him.

"And as he sat upon the mount of Olives, the disciples came unto him privately, saying, Tell us, when shall these things be? and what shall be the sign of thy coming, and of the end of the world?" (Matthew 24:3)

All true disciples of Jesus will inquire of Him. They will come to Him, even if they're alone, and ask for His wisdom and revelation concerning the future. They understand that they need His revelation and guidance to be able to fulfill their purpose and destiny and to be in sync with the Lord's times and seasons.

"But when his disciples saw it, they had indignation, saying, To what purpose is this waste?" (Matthew 26:8)

At times disciples will misunderstand acts of love toward the Lord. They will look at it as insignificant or a waste but as they remain around the Lord and walk closely with Him, He will shift their value system until it becomes just like His.

"Now the first day of the feast of unleavened bread the disciples came to Jesus, saying unto him, Where wilt thou that we prepare for thee to eat the passover?" (Matthew 26:17)

Christ's disciples will prepare a place for Him to rest and commune with them. Just like John the Baptist said, we must prepare the way of The Lord. He is a King and He is Royal and must be treated as such. That is called honor.

"And he said, Go into the city to such a man, and say unto him, The Master saith, My time is at hand; I will keep the passover at thy house with my disciples." (Matthew 26:18)

The disciples of Jesus will relay His Royal Decrees. They will speak on behalf of the King, in His stead.

"And as they were eating, Jesus took bread, and blessed it, and brake it, and gave it to the disciples, and said, Take, eat; this is my body." (Matthew 26:26)

The Lord will share Himself with His disciples. He will give us bread from Heaven, which is His body, that gives us eternal life. That is the revelation of The Lord's prayer when Jesus says *"give us this day our daily bread."* He was requesting a daily Impartation of Himself for His disciples. If we were to quote this request in light of this revelation we would say *"give us this day our daily **Jesus**."*

"Peter said unto him, Though I should die with thee, yet will I not deny thee. Likewise also said all the disciples." (Matthew 26:35)

In our relationship with Jesus, at times He will tell us hard truths about ourselves. We must be humble enough to receive and submit to His truth about us because it is just that, *truth!* Also, discipleship requires allegiance. This type of relationship with Jesus is a Covenant of Faithfulness.

"Then cometh Jesus with them unto a place called Gethsemane, and saith unto the disciples, Sit ye here, while I go and pray yonder." (Matthew 26:36)

There will be times of stillness and waiting on The Lord as a disciple. There is a great deal of patience that is required to be a disciple of Jesus Christ. Impatience will always cause us to get out of the will of God.

"And he cometh unto the disciples, and findeth them asleep, and saith unto Peter, What, could ye not watch with me one hour?" (Matthew 26:40)

Accountability and dependability are two essential attributes of being a disciple. The Lord will require these of us but is also merciful when we fall short. He is good to us!

"Then cometh he to his disciples, and saith unto them, Sleep on now, and take your rest: behold, the hour is at hand, and the Son of man is betrayed into the hands of sinners." (Matthew 26:45)

There are things that the Lord does require us to deal with as disciples. There are also things that He has ordained to handle Himself and He wants us to rest in Him during those times. Trusting in Him to take care of those things.

"But all this was done, that the scriptures of the prophets might be fulfilled. Then all the disciples forsook him, and fled." (Matthew 26:56)

When Jesus is doing a hard thing to fulfill righteousness, there are disciples who will forsake Him and flee. But just like for the disciples in the Bible, there is restoration if we return to Him.

"When the even was come, there came a rich man of Arimathaea, named Joseph, who also himself was Jesus' disciple" (Matthew 27:57)

There will be some disciples that go unnoticed. Some may even have great status and clout, but they are true disciples. (*I will elaborate more on this subject later*)

"And go quickly, and tell his disciples that he is risen from the dead; and, behold, he goeth before you into Galilee; there shall ye see him: lo, I have told you." (Matthew 28:7)

Disciples will be given revelation of what Jesus is doing. They will receive prophetic revelation and instruction so that they can be in sync with The Lord.

"Saying, Say ye, His disciples came by night, and stole him away while we slept." (Matthew 28:13)

Disciples will at times be lied on and slandered. This comes with the territory of being a disciple of Jesus.

"Then the eleven disciples went away into Galilee, into a mountain where Jesus had appointed them." (Matthew 28:16)

Disciples will walk in unity. This unity will cause them to ascend spiritually and be where The Lord desires them to be.

Chapter Glossary

Ascend - to move up or climb something.

Allegiance - loyalty and support for a ruler, country, group, or belief.

Brethren - (used as a form of address to members of an organization or religious group) brothers.

Notes

Notes

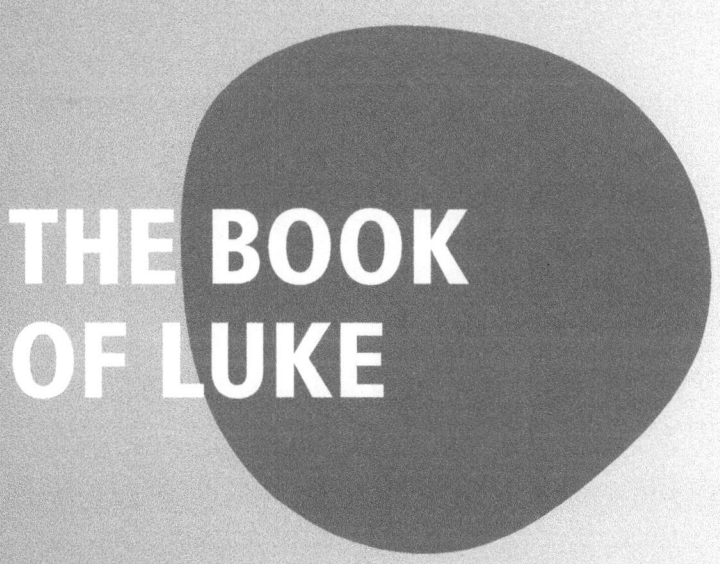

THE BOOK OF LUKE

"And when it was day, he called unto him his disciples: and of them he chose twelve, whom also he named apostles." (Luke 6:13)

Disciples must be called by Jesus Himself. You cannot make yourself a disciple. You must be called to be a disciple and once called to be a disciple, you must answer the call. Then after answering the call, you will be sent out. The good news is that Jesus has called every believer to be his disciple!

"And he came down with them, and stood in the plain, and the company of his disciples, and a great multitude of people out of all Judaea and Jerusalem, and from the sea coast of Tyre and Sidon, which came to

hear him, and to be healed of their diseases." (Luke 6:17)

Disciples will stand with Jesus in his healing ministry. They will be extensions of Jesus' healing authority and power in the earth and manifest Him. To be a part of the healing ministry of Jesus, we as disciples must stand as healers in His stead.

"And he lifted up his eyes on his disciples, and said, Blessed be ye poor: for yours is the kingdom of God." (Luke 6:20)

It is so important for the disciples of Jesus to have Face-to-face revelation and teaching from The Lord. This is what revolutionizes disciples and trains them more effectively than anything else in the Kingdom of God. But this type of relationship will only come through humility or being *poor* in spirit.

"The disciple is not above his master: but every one that is perfect shall be as his master." (Luke 6:40)

This is and should be the goal of every disciple of Jesus Christ. Which is to be like Him in every way! When the verse says "perfect" it is actually saying "mature" and "complete." So every disciple that has come into full maturity will be like Jesus, who is complete. (Colossians 2:10)

"And his disciples asked him, saying, What might this parable be?" (Luke 8:9)

All disciples must fight for pride in their own understanding, especially being close to The Lord. They cannot presume on the Lord's understanding thinking because they are close to Him, that their thoughts are his thoughts or their understanding his understanding. They must always ask for the Lord's revelation. (Proverbs 3:5)

"Then he called his twelve disciples together, and gave them power and authority over all devils, and to cure diseases." (Luke 9:1)

Disciples have been given authority from Jesus to cast out devils and heal the sick. It is a kingdom inheritance for all those who receive Jesus. It is a part of the disciple's kingship. (St. John 1:12)

"And it came to pass, as he was alone praying, his disciples were with him: and he asked them, saying, Whom say the people that I am?" (Luke 9:18)

Jesus will make sure His disciples are certain of His identity. His identity as the only begotten Son of God, God in flesh and the Living Word of God must be established in the heart of every disciple. We must know His identity and personality if we're going to be like Him. This revelation of Who Jesus is, is also a protection for demonic and satanic deception.

"And I besought thy disciples to cast him out; and they could not." (Luke 9:40)

Disciples will learn the mysteries and revelations of authority and power. This will come through failures at times but Jesus is always ready to show His disciples how to be successful in the future.

"And when his disciples James and John saw this, they said, Lord, wilt thou that we command fire to come

down from heaven, and consume them, even as Elias did?" (Luke 9:54)

There are times when disciples' hearts must be turned by The Lord. To love the way He loves and to have compassion the way he has compassion. To be a disciple of Jesus Christ you must carry his redemptive heart and love for souls.

"And he turned him unto his disciples, and said privately, Blessed are the eyes which see the things that ye see." (Luke 10:23)

There are special blessings and revelations that the disciples of The Lord receive that the masses do not. Their eyes are opened to receive and understand the mysteries of the Kingdom of God. They receive this because of their closeness to the Lord. While others don't have access to this privilege because they have not paid the price to be His disciples.

"And it came to pass, that, as he was praying in a certain place, when he ceased, one of his disciples said unto him, Lord, teach us to pray, as John also taught his disciples." (Luke 11:1)

Jesus will instruct his disciples in the art of prayer. He will teach them the proper and correct protocol for approaching His Father in prayer. (Matthew 6:13)

"In the mean time, when there were gathered together an innumerable multitude of people, insomuch that they trode one upon another, he began to say unto his disciples first of all, Beware ye of the leaven of the Pharisees, which is hypocrisy." (Luke 12:1)

Disciples will often receive warnings from the Lord. Warnings that will keep them safe from falling into the traps and devices of satan. These warnings from The Lord will preserve your future and destiny.

"And he said unto his disciples, Therefore I say unto you, Take no thought for your life, what ye shall eat; neither for the body, what ye shall put on." (Luke 12:22)

There is a faith that is required of disciples that removes the effect of the cares of this life. This faith in the Lord for their daily provision keeps them in perfect peace. Disciples grow in this daily as they continue to walk with the Lord.

"And he said also unto his disciples, There was a certain rich man, which had a steward; and the same was accused unto him that he had wasted his goods." (Luke 16:1)

Jesus will speak to His disciples in parables in order to exercise, sharpen, and strengthen their discernment. To heighten their spiritual senses to be in tune with Him and what He is saying.

"And he said unto the disciples, The days will come, when ye shall desire to see one of the days of the Son of man, and ye shall not see it." (Luke 17:22)

There are times of extreme closeness with the Lord and there are times or seasons of distance. Though He never leaves or forsakes us, He will distance or quiet Himself in order to test and ignite your passion for Him in a much deeper way. He desires us to literally **seek His Face!**

"And it came to pass, when he was come nigh to Bethphage and Bethany, at the mount called the mount of Olives, he sent two of his disciples. Saying, Go ye into the village over against you; in the which at your entering ye shall find a colt tied, whereon yet never man sat: loose him, and bring him hither. And if any man ask you, Why do ye loose him? thus shall ye say unto him, Because the Lord hath need of him.(Luke 19:29-31)

The disciples of Christ will at times help Him in fulfilling prophecy. He will give them assignments to complete that will help fulfill His word and His divine will in the earth.

"And when he was come nigh, even now at the descent of the mount of Olives, the whole multitude of the disciples began to rejoice and praise God with a loud voice for all the mighty works that they had seen." (Luke 19:37)

Praise must be in the heart of every disciple. It is, along with worship, a heart softener and a faith builder. Praise sets God as our focus and magnifies Him before our eyes. It is indeed due Him and right that He be praised and glorified, especially by His disciples. Praise also brings Him closer to us. (Psalms 22:3)

"And some of the Pharisees from among the multitude said unto him, Master, rebuke thy disciples." (Luke 19:39)

Many times people will believe or feel that the Lord should deal with His disciples in a certain way. But at the end of the day, He is their master and will deal with them as He pleases. According to His divine wisdom.

"Then in the audience of all the people he said unto his disciples." (Luke 20:25)

There are times where The Lord will openly address His disciples among the audiences of people. He will publicly address them with whatever message He desires for them to receive. Disciples must be willing at times to be publicly addressed.

"And ye shall say unto the goodman of the house, The Master saith unto thee, Where is the guest chamber, where I shall eat the passover with my disciples?" (Luke 22:11)

Jesus looks for and sets up opportunities to have communion and fellowship with His disciples. He will even use others to help set up this fellowship between His disciples and Himself.

"And when he rose up from prayer, and was come to his disciples, he found them sleeping for sorrow." (Luke 22:45)

This is literally a wake-up call for all disciples. Jesus who is our intercessor is always praying and working on our behalf. We as disciples have to join Him in His work and plan in our lives. As disciples, we co-labor with Him in fulfilling the will of God, and we have to be spiritually *awake* to do this.

Notes

Notes

_____

_____

_____

_____

_____

_____

_____

_____

_____

_____

_____

Chapter Glossary

Identity - a person's name and other facts about who they are.

Intercession - the act of using your influence to make someone in authority forgive someone else or save them from punishment.

Parables - a short, simple story that teaches or explains an idea, especially a moral or religious idea.

THE HIDDEN DISCIPLES

"When the even was come, there came a rich man of Arimathaea, named Joseph, who also himself was Jesus' disciple: He went to Pilate, and begged the body of Jesus. Then Pilate commanded the body to be delivered. And when Joseph had taken the body, he wrapped it in a clean linen cloth, And laid it in his own new tomb, which he had hewn out in the rock: and he rolled a great stone to the door of the sepulchre, and departed." (Matthew 27:57-60)

We must understand that every disciple of Jesus Christ will not be openly or widely known. There are some disciples who follow Him in secret.

They will not be your normal everyday

Sunday morning Christian. They will be major businessmen, actors, artists, musicians, professional athletes, etc. These people to the masses will be known for their profession or career. They will not be known at large as disciples of The Lord Jesus Christ. Because of the pull of their natural lives, their ever-increasing closeness and fellowship with The Lord will be primarily in the secret place. In the late hours of the night and in the early morning before The Lord, is where these hidden disciples will be found.

They will be like Nicodemus in St.John 3:1-2 which says *"There was a man of the Pharisees, named Nicodemus, a ruler of the Jews: The same came to Jesus by night..."* Their personal time with The Lord will be their greatest possession. These will be some of the most earnest followers and disciples of Jesus Christ. Though their relationship with Him will mostly be hidden from the masses, it will be a relationship of intense passion and intimacy. With the burning desire and humility to be taught by Jesus, they will *make time* to spend with Him, even to their own inconvenience. Many of these will be the hidden push behind many of the last-day ministries and ministers God will bring onto the scene. They'll fund the Kingdom of God in a radical and ridiculous way because of their relationship with Jesus Christ. These men and women will also turn their spheres of influence upside down with the message of the Kingdom of God, bringing many influential people to Christ in these last days.

It is one of the strategies of the enemy to turn us

against those with influence, power, and money. This is because he knows that it is the Will of God to use these men and women to bless, support, and provide for His body. Just like the disciple Joseph did, they too will *provide* for the Body of Christ. They will open doors for the Body of Christ and they will help preserve the Body of Christ. We must be wise and win these men and women of influence, these future disciples of Jesus Christ because the Lord has great plans for them.

Chapter Glossary

Passion - a very powerful feeling, for example of sexual attraction, love, hate, anger, or other emotion.

Humility - the quality of not being proud because you are aware of your bad qualities.

Influence - the power to have an effect on people or things, or a person or thing that is able to do this.

Notes

Notes

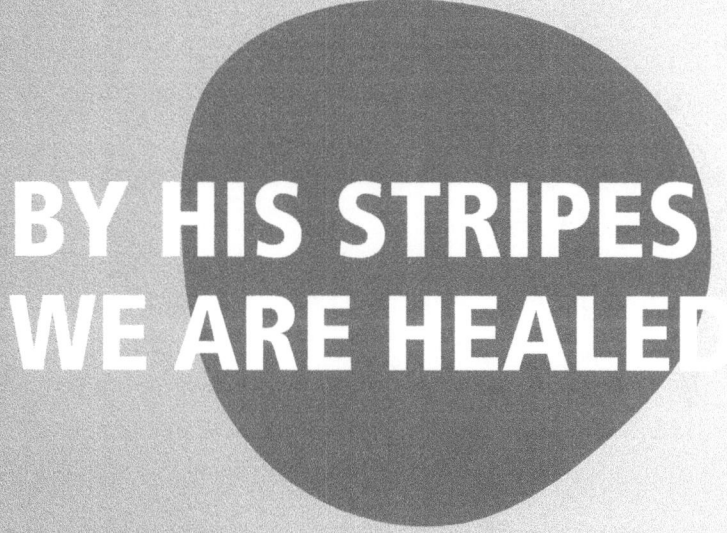

BY HIS STRIPES WE ARE HEALED

Isaiah 53:5 KJVS

But he was wounded for our transgressions, he was bruised for our iniquities: the chastisement of our peace was upon him; and with his stripes we are healed.

This is a scripture that many Christians are familiar with and rejoice in, but there is another revelation to this verse. Many think and reminisce on this scripture during the time of the Passover. We often think of the physical and mental suffering of the Lord and what He had to endure. We often rejoice over the benefits we have received as a result of His sacrifice. But there is more revelation to be unlocked in this scripture than meets the eye.

As a disciple of the Lord, it is evident that there is discipline involved in this relationship. The word disciple is derived from the word *discipline*. So to be a disciple is to also be a disciplined one.

As I was in prayer one morning I was listening to a song as I prayed. The song quoted the scripture saying by his stripes we are healed. As I was praying and listening to the song the Lord spoke to me. He said, "There is another revelation to that scripture." Then He said, "By MY stripes you are healed." There was an explosion of illumination in my spirit. I understood He was saying that by the chastisement He gives us, we are healed from the spiritual ailments in our character and nature. The scripture says in Proverbs 3:11-12 *"My son, despise not the chastening of the Lord; neither be weary of his correction: For whom the Lord loveth he correcteth; even as a father the son in whom he delighteth."* In other words, it is by His stripes (His chastening) that we are healed from the wickedness in us. He sets us free and heals us from spiritual disease by correcting us through his chastening.

This is also evident in Luke 12:47 which says *"And that servant, which knew his lord's will, and prepared not himself, neither did according to his will, shall be beaten with many stripes."* Just like the lashes the Lord took on our behalf that lacerated his flesh, He lacerates us. He uses life, circumstances, trials, and even people as *his whip* to lacerate us and cause bad blood (iniquities) to flow out of us. Iniquities are passed down through our bloodline (Exodus

34:7). They are literal blood diseases that we carry until freed from them by the Lord. The lacerations of the Lord open us up spiritually and expose the iniquity hidden within us and our character. That left alone, would've most likely never been revealed. Therefore leaving us spiritually sick with iniquities even though we may look well. Even in the case that they are exposed, if we do not deal with them and allow the Lord's free course to cleanse and heal us, they will eventually ruin us. This chastening is a deep testimony to the depth of God's love for us. He loves us so much that He wants to set us completely free of all ailments both physical and spiritual. He wants to make us whole body, soul, and spirit. As His disciples, we must submit ourselves to this wonderful manifestation of His love. Though it is painful, it is necessary and liberating. It is the healing power of God working in our lives to set us free from every disease, ailment, and flaw in us as a result of the fall. This is a huge part of how we are perfected and transformed into His image and likeness. We as His disciples desperately need this to be like Him. *By his stripes we are Healed!*

Chapter Glossary

Transformed - having been changed in an important way.

Reminisce - to talk or write about past experiences that you remember with pleasure.

Liberating - making you feel free and able to behave as you like.

Notes

Notes

THE SCIENCE OF THE HOLY SPIRIT

"And it shall come to pass afterward, that I will pour out my spirit upon all flesh; and your sons and your daughters shall prophesy, your old men shall dream dreams, your young men shall see visions." (Joel 2:28)

In this passage of scripture, we see by revelation that there are three distinct ways for the manifestation of the outpouring of The Spirit. In Acts 2:4 we read *"And they were all filled with the Holy Ghost, and began to speak with other tongues, as the Spirit gave them utterance."* So in context, we see that the initial evidence of the Infilling of the Holy Spirit is to speak with other tongues, as the Spirit gives utterance. But as we just read in

Joel 2:28 we see that there are three avenues for this manifestation. These avenues are prophecy (inspired utterance), dreams, and visions. Let's examine!

We will start with prophecy. What is prophecy in its simplest form? Well, in 1 Corinthians 14:3, it says *"But he that prophesieth **speaketh** unto men to **edification, and exhortation, and comfort."** So here we see that prophecy in its simplest form is inspired words of edification, exhortation, and comfort given by The Spirit of God. This (prophecy) happens in all languages of the earth. That's what the scripture meant when it said *"and began to speak with other tongues."* They were not speaking words in another language with no substance, but were under the Spirit's unction and utterance, speaking words of edification, exhortation and comfort in languages foreign to them. Now there is a dimension of prophecy that pertains to the foretelling of the future by the Spirit, but here we are speaking of prophecy in its simplicity. You see, when you are filled with the Holy Spirit you will speak in another language that you are not familiar with and that you don't know. So in essence you will *prophesy* in another language. This is found in Acts 2:6 where it says *"Now when this was noised abroad, the multitude came together, and were confounded, because that every man heard them speak in his own language."* This multitude heard those in the upper room speaking by the utterance of the Spirit in their native languages and were confounded. To dive a little deeper, in Revelation 19:10 we read that *"the testimony of Jesus is the spirit of prophecy."* Then in St. John 16:13 Jesus says *"Howbeit when he, the **Spirit of** *truth, is come, he will guide you into all truth: for he shall not speak of himself; but whatsoever he shall hear, that shall he speak: and he will shew you things to come.*" So from these two passages of scripture, we see that the Spirit only prophesies (speaks words of edification, exhortation, and comfort) what He hears from Jesus, which is what the scripture calls the *testimony of Jesus.* Which we just read is the *spirit of prophecy.* So when a believer is baptized in the Holy Ghost the utterance that comes forth out of them is *the testimony of Jesus* which is *spirit of prophecy!*

Another great example of speaking in tongues and prophecy being linked together in the initial Infilling of The Holy Spirit is Acts 19:6 which states *"And when Paul had laid his hands upon them, the Holy Ghost came on them; and they* **spake with tongues, and prophesied."**

Now I must clarify that there is a difference between sign tongues, which occur as a sign at the initial Infilling of the Holy Spirit in the life of a believer and unknown tongues which are tongues that are for communication between GOD and the believer speaking only. This manifestation of tongues is referenced in 1 Corinthians 14:2 stating *"For he that speaketh in an* **unknown tongue** *speaketh not unto men,* **but unto God:** *for no man understandeth him; howbeit in the spirit he speaketh mysteries."* But the initial sign on a believer when they are filled with the Holy Spirit is to speak in *other tongues,* which equates to prophesying in another language not known to the believer. So this is the parallel of the first category of the Spirit being poured out on believers and them prophesying. When they receive the Holy Spirit they speak in other tongues (prophesy) as the Spirit gives utterance, but they have no visions, and they are not in a dream.

Another manifestation of the Infilling of the Holy Spirit mentioned in the scripture, is accompanied by visions. Visions are spiritual pictures, images, scenes, and experiences that God reveals through opening the spiritual eyes. Now we must understand that there are three levels of visionary experiences: spiritual (internal) visions, trances, and open visions. Spiritual visions are visions that are experienced through the mind's eye or internally. These are visions that we mostly experience when our eyes are *closed*. An example of this is in Acts 9:3-6,8 where The Apostle Paul was converted to Christ through a visionary experience on the road to Damascus. It reads *"And as he journeyed, he came near Damascus: and suddenly there shined round about him a light from heaven: And he fell to the earth, and heard a voice saying unto him, Saul, Saul, why persecutest thou me? And he said, Who art thou, Lord? And the Lord said, I am Jesus whom thou persecutest: it is hard for thee to kick against the pricks. And he trembling and astonished said, Lord, what wilt thou have me to do? And the Lord said unto him, Arise, and go into the city, and it shall be told thee what thou must do. And Saul arose from the earth; and* **when his eyes were opened***, he saw no man: but they led him by the hand, and brought him into Damascus."* We see here that this was an internal vision because it says that *when his eyes were opened.* He saw this vision of the Lord Jesus internally. This is validated by Acts 9:7 which says *"And the men which journeyed with him stood speechless, hearing a voice, but **seeing no man.**"* This vision was internal and personal to the Apostle Paul.

Then we have trances which are visions in which the physical senses are suspended for a time, these also often happen internally or when the eyes are closed. There is often a sense of being taken to another place or being engulfed in the atmosphere of your visionary experience. As previously stated, in trances your physical senses are suspended or less tangible as the spiritual realm becomes the dominant atmosphere. A great example of a trance visionary experience is also in Acts 10:9-10 where it says, *"On the morrow, as they went on their journey, and drew nigh unto the city, Peter went up upon the housetop to pray about the sixth hour: And he became very hungry, and would have eaten: but while they made ready, he fell into a **trance.**"* Peter later testified of this experience saying in Acts 11:15 *"I was in the city of Joppa praying: and in a **trance** I saw a vision, A certain vessel descend, as it had been a great sheet, let down from heaven by four corners; and it came even to me."* The Apostle Peter clearly stated he was in a trance and saw a vision. This validates through scripture that visions through being in a trance-like state are a manifestation of the Spirit of God and can be used by Him in filling a believer. One more example of this level of vision is also in Acts. Where the Apostle Paul says by The Spirit *"And it came to pass, that, when I was come again to Jerusalem, even while I prayed in the temple, I was in* a **trance**; *And saw him saying unto me, Make haste, and get thee quickly out of Jerusalem: for they will not receive thy testimony concerning me.*" (Acts 22:17-18) There is a parallel between the two trances in scripture we just mentioned and it is *prayer*. Prayer is great way to experience visions from God!

The last and greatest level of vision is the open vision. The open vision is experienced when the eyes are open and the spiritual realm appears just like the natural realm. It becomes just as apparent and real as the natural realm, and sometimes dulls the senses of the natural realm and heightens the senses of the spiritual realm. Some have said it's like watching a movie screen and I believe this is a great analogy of these types of visions. Some open visions go beyond what we just stated and totally consume the natural realm around you and all you see and since is the spiritual realm. There are many examples of this in scripture, especially in the book of Revelation. One great example of an open vision is in Isaiah 6 when the prophet Isaiah had an open vision of The Lord in the temple sitting on His Throne high and lifted up. For him, it was as if this were in the natural realm but it was an open vision and impartation given to him by God. These three types of visions are all ways that the Holy Spirit can manifest and baptize a believer, accompanied by and with the evidence of speaking in other tongues.

The last way that the scripture says the Spirit of God can fill (baptize) a believer is through dreams. Dreams are the visions of the night as it says in scripture.

They are revelation and impartation from God given while you're sleeping. We see in 1 Kings 3:5 where it says "In Gibeon the Lord appeared to Solomon in a dream by night: and God said, Ask what I shall give thee." So we see here that God gives gifts and grants requests in and through dreams. Solomon, in this case, asked for wisdom and it was imparted to him by God in and through the dream. Then he awoke from the dream with the spirit of wisdom and became the wisest man in the world. This is the same when it comes to being filled or baptized in the Holy Spirit. Jesus said in Luke 11:13 *"...how much more shall your heavenly Father give the Holy Spirit to them that ask him?"* And once you ask him it will happen in one of these three avenues mentioned in Joel 2:28. Which are prophecy (spirit utterance only in other tongues), visions (visionary experience w/speaking in other tongues), or dreams (night visions w/speaking in other tongues). The dream realm is so fun because it introduces us to the creativity of God all while we're asleep. God has filled many believers with His Spirit through dreams. I've heard cases where the person dreaming sees themselves being filled with the Spirit or has an encounter with The Lord in the dream. In many cases when they come to themselves or wake up, they're speaking in tongues in the natural realm!

That being said it is of great importance that every believer seeks to speak in tongues as often as possible, because of its benefits. It builds up and charges your spirit man and gives you a direct line of communication with GOD. It also brings inner healing, transformation, and deliverance to the believer. It is a faith builder, as well as giving the believer a greater capacity for revelation and mysteries by enhancing their understanding. Speaking in tongues often also helps increase the anointing on your life to operate in the supernatural (healings, deliverance, prophecy, etc). It is of great importance that every believer and disciple of Jesus Christ be filled with the Holy Spirit. Without the Holy Spirit, it is impossible to follow Jesus the way that He desires us to. It is also impossible to be transformed into His Image without the Holy Spirit. It is He, the *Holy* Spirit that enables us to live *holy* and consecrated to the Lord. The Holy Spirit also brings to life the very words of Jesus, He illuminates them so that we receive proper revelation and instruction from them. It is by the communion of the Holy Spirit that we fellowship with God and that He is revealed to us. He is our dearest and closest companion in this life given to us by The Lord Himself. We all must receive the gift of (the Person) the Holy Spirit. He is God's down payment to us for our eternal dwelling place with Him in Heaven. As Jesus told the disciples ***"Receive ye the Holy Ghost."***

Chapter Glossary

Visionary - a person who is able to imagine how a country, society, industry, etc., will or should develop in the future and to plan in a suitable way.

Edification - the improvement of the mind and understanding, especially by learning.

Exhortation - the act of strongly encouraging or trying to persuade someone to do something.

Notes

Notes

Notes

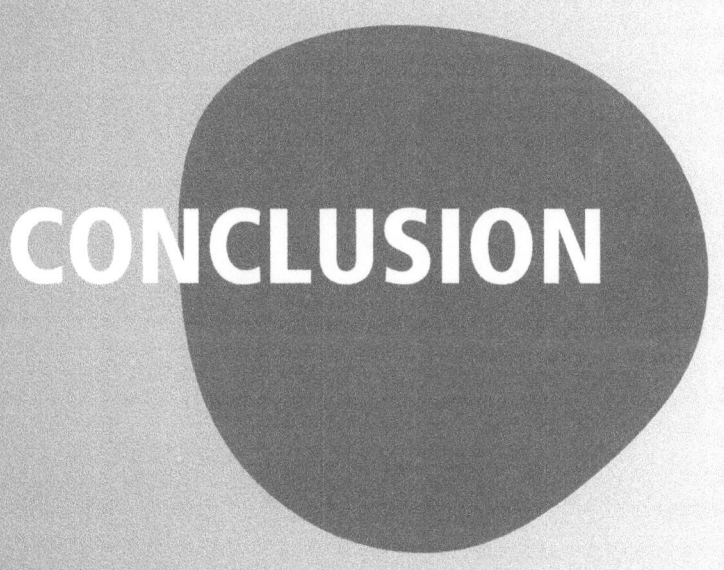

CONCLUSION

My prayer is that this book has ignited a passionate pursuit in you to be a disciple of Jesus Christ. That your eyes have been opened and your spirit man expanded by the revelation and teaching given to me by the Spirit of God. That at the conclusion of this book, there would be one more disciple added to Jesus Christ!

Notes

Notes

Notes

Notes

Notes

Notes

ABOUT THE AUTHOR

Paige Michael Williams is a minister of the Gospel of Jesus Christ from northeast Ohio. God speaks to him by revelation through dreams and visions, as well as prophetically. In 2017 He was given a commission by The Lord to "Write down what you hear." This book is just a small fulfillment of that commission.

Other titles by this Author:

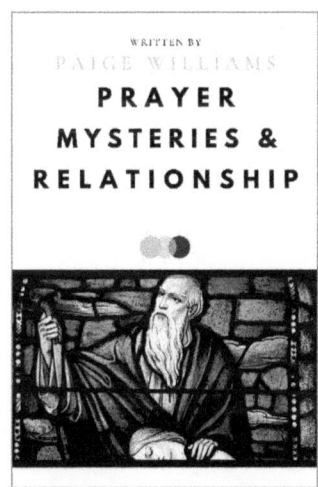

Seraph Creative is a collective of artists, writers, theologians & illustrators who desire to see the body of Christ grow into full maturity, walking in their inheritance as Sons of God on the Earth.

Sign up to our newsletter to know about future exciting releases.

Visit our website :

www.seraphcreative.org

www.ingramcontent.com/pod-product-compliance
Lightning Source LLC
Chambersburg PA
CBHW051544120626
46551CB00013B/1367